Be...a Woman

expressions of life

First published in Canada in 2007
by Beautiful Beginnings Youth Inc.
Toronto, Canada
www.be-awoman.com

2007 2008 2009 2010 / 10 9 8 7 6 5 4 3 2 1

Printed and bound in Canada by Friesens

Library and Archives Canada Cataloguing in Publication

MacGregor, Kim, 1968-
Be...a Woman: expressions of life/by Kim MacGregor & Arline Malakian.
ISBN 978-0-9731301-5-7
1. Women--Conduct of life. 2. Women--Psychology.
I. Malakian, Arline, 1960- II. Title.
HQ1206.M33 2007   158.1082   C2007-904750-5

Project Editor: Dan Varrette

Visit us on the Web at: www.be-awoman.com
Contact us with "Be a Woman" in the subject line at: info@be-awoman.com

design by Sharon Snider
Copplestone Works
Contact us with "Design" in the subject line
at: copplestone.works@sympatico.ca

It has been a transforming experience creating this book with Arline. I use the word *create* because that was the key energy driving every element of this collaboration. We have created friendships, revelations, and new definitions for women and beauty. Although Arline, the photographer, and I, the writer, adhere to our individual designations, it was through endless hours of discussing, analyzing, experiencing, and comparing our own unique lives that we developed a shared philosophy about what it truly means to be a woman. This meaning is the philosophy of the book, which propels it in so many directions and allows us to feel such a myriad of emotions. Arline and I live vastly different lives, yet we share many similarities. For all that we share and no matter how we differ, we exist as women. In the process of creating this book, we have discovered that all women share many inherent qualities that make each of us, and all of us, who we are.

The heart of this project was the desire to create a wonderful gift for women to experience and acknowledge — something within which they can and should rejoice. Being a woman is so complex and meaningful. Unfortunately, at times, and in certain parts of the world today, being a woman has been reduced to "only" or "less than," but it is "more" than so many things. Being a woman is more than the sum of one's parts: breasts, hair, lips, and legs. It is more than beauty — more than the outside, more than the inside. It is more than age — more than young, more than old. It is more than skin color — more than white, black, or brown. It is more than body type — more than thin or full figured, more than short or tall. It is more than being a mother, sister, lover, or friend. Because women are so diverse, being a woman is difficult to describe with images alone. It is also difficult to describe with words alone. We chose to express being a woman by combining images with words, honestly, so that we can glimpse into the soul of womanhood.

Arline and I have had the absolute privilege of meeting some remarkable women of the world, some of whom are represented in this book. Everywhere we look, we see women that light up the room, the street, the café they occupy. They don't match the models that Arline is accustomed to meeting at fashion shoots, or those I know from auditions and castings. Rather, they comprise the rest of the entire population of phenomenal women quietly living extraordinary lives. **This book is a result of many phenomenal people whom we are grateful to have in our lives.**

Acknowledgments from Arline

Thank you to my dad for his unconditional love and support and for his inspirational example of humanity in all aspects of life; my sister for who she is: a quiet, and constant source of patience, wisdom, and faith; Laura Alaimo, who was a force in prompting me to inspire others with my beliefs; Leora Eisen and Leanna Crouch, who were the first to actively launch me in this "beauty quest," and to Dove, who created the arena for it; all my relationships and life experiences, past and present, that have contributed to who I am; Anoush Sahakian, whose time and devotion to this project inspired me to create the template for the look and feel of the images; Kim, my partner, my friend, whose lightness and drive I cherish and without whom this book would not have been. Thanks to her poetry that gave life to immortal moments of connections, to her magical words that express gently, honestly, and inclusively all that I believe in, and to the beauty we discovered together.

Acknowledgments from Kim

Thank you to my husband and soulmate, who has supported and encouraged Arline and me throughout this entire process in a multitude of ways and with whom I am delighted to be sharing my journey in life; my three beautiful, creative, enthusiastic little girls, who inspire me to want to change the world for the next generation of women; my sister, who has taught me so much about being a woman through her advice and unwavering support during both my triumphs and challenges; my brother, whose journey in life, spirituality, and soul searching inspire me immensely; my surrogate mother, the best mother-in-law a girl could hope for, who reveled in the daily bits of excitement I shared with her along the way and who was always there, with love and treats for my girls; Jodi Rademeyer, whose friendship, encouragement, and help with my children when I ran late to pick up the kids from school reinforced the message of real beauty we were creating; Maggie Mills, who graciously and enthusiastically took the time to edit all our work from the book proposal to the introduction; two special friends Erika and Paula; and Arline, a generous partner and a treasured friend, whom I deeply admire for her unparalleled creative vision that guided this project, and her emotional, stunning still photos that stir the senses and spur imagination. Her words inspired me throughout this experience with a philosophy I have been delighted to both share in and grow from.

Acknowledgments from Both of Us

Thank you to Jackie Gideon for bringing us together; Kelly Harms for her interest and belief in us and in our project; Frank Miraglia, an amazing mentor whose words of advice and encouragement helped push this project along; Sharon Snider, our amazing designer who was instrumental in bringing our images and words to life on paper, for her exquisite sense of design, for her "getting us" and our message, and for being the wise and solid soundboard; Michael Penney, our videographer from After Light Films, for his calm presence and sincere interest in our work; and the phenomenal real women whose faces grace the pages of this book and who shared a segment of their lives with us. Their stories all have a place in our hearts. **To all who supported this project, we thank you!**

Be...aWoman

expressions of life

Have you ever gazed at a woman, feeling yourself breathe free of judgment and preconceived ideals and found beauty in her face? Has that feeling ever led you to the desire to know more about her? Everyone has a story to tell. Sometimes we can read a chapter of the story in a face but rarely the whole novella. The beauty of womanhood cannot be found in any form of perfection but rather in the truth of existence. Whom does she love? Who loves her? What has she dealt with? How has she struggled? How has she triumphed? Who is she being? We find ourselves longing to know the stories of their lives so we can touch their essence, so we can feel connected to this amazing group of women for whom we have such deep respect and in whose community we are grateful to be members.

Since we began working on *Be...a Woman* Arline and I found ourselves on a journey we had not fully anticipated. Though the idea of showing images of real women and discovering the individual attributes that help to define their beauty was our primary ambition, we had no idea how much we would learn about ourselves and how deeply we would fall in love with the process of learning more about strangers. Living the experience of creating this book has far exceeded our greatest expectations. Allowing each moment to unfold, we discovered our own true potential and ease. Creating this book became a thrilling exercise of living consciously in every moment.

During our initial meeting, Arline and I discussed the process of choosing attributes and matching them with people we met who seemed to best represent each attribute. Before we even transferred our thoughts to paper, we looked at each other for a moment, realizing intuitively that this project had to move ahead on its own, with freedom and a sense of discovery. We chose not to choose. We created an environment in which each woman was heard, seen, and acknowledged for her individual presence and being. We did not care about where she came from, the size of her waist, or her age. We cared about who she was.

It felt like many of these moments where an exploration of self, a chance for all of us to access our conscious level of being, not the persona we project to the world: full of masks, critical thoughts, and judgments, rather than the elegantly simple beings who embrace one another's spirits and make it okay to just be ourselves. Because of that freedom, each photo shoot became a lesson for us all. There were exchanges of stories and ideas, advice and wisdom, heart and soul — true expressions of life. With each moment with every woman, stories flowed so organically without any preconceived ideas about who would be photographed for which attribute. It was only after spending time with each woman and then seeing the magical images Arline captured that the pages really came to life.

By observing — in really stopping the whole crazy train of life and being still, quiet, and present, listening to these women speak — we learned so many things. Most important, we discovered how we rarely take the time to truly find out about someone else, and in so doing, discover things about ourselves. As women, perhaps we need to draw more from our shared experiences than from the desire to be "better than," "thinner than," or "more successful than." Casting aside the limitations and inadequacies that haunt us, whether defined by the media or self-induced by rigidly categorizing our entire lives by what we consider to be our "story," we discover that we are more than what we think we are. We tune in to the abundant energy that surrounds us, moves in us, with us, even beyond us and beyond our stories, in a limitless flow of evolution. We are less critical of ourselves, less critical of others, and more accepting of all forms of beauty. Beauty is contagious: it transforms us, and we, in turn, transform those around us. We recognize that we are complete and we shine. Celebrating the beauty in others has a rippling effect as they shine, radiating back to us. Bathing in the warmth of admiration and value, we rid ourselves of false, immobilizing expectations. We are enough! No justification needed...no excuses! We can all shine! We are all beautiful! Beauty is contagious!

This book is a reminder of what is truly beautiful and that we need not search endlessly to find beauty. We have all that we need within ourselves to live a life of love and happiness. We are trained, however, to identify with our outer selves: a name...a story...how others perceive us...what we own...the way we look — only to still feel that constant internal pang of emptiness.   Arline and I learned and continue to learn about the power of our true selves, our core. We simply need to look inside us to that sweet, special soul that abounds with such wonder. It sits quietly poised, waiting to make its acquaintance all over again as we learn to marvel at it, at our own brilliance. At the core of every one of us is the magical, eternal life force that is energy and love — it is our source. In synchronicity with all others and nature, this force is complete, generative, creative, and beautiful. This book is a celebration of the connection with our true selves — with our being...fully — in joy, trust, and freedom.

The images we are sharing with you are captured in these "moments of being." We shared the simplicity of our intent with the women we met. We saw them as beautiful. In turn, they gave us the gift of feeling honored. What we shared was true and raw and right to the source of being. None of us were caught up in trying to impress one another; we were simply caught up "in each other," in the essence of being that filled the room. So simple, really, and yet, as you will see in the images, so very beautiful.

By softening our gaze at ourselves and at others and allowing for a more all-encompassing view of what it truly means to *be a woman*, we experienced being connected in a fullness of life beyond thinking. It is a feeling of complete fulfillment and gratitude. Whether we are walking down the street or standing in line at the bank or grocery store, regardless of where we are, perhaps this book will allow all of us to pause and engage in the true possibilities of life. In sharing a smile, laughing together with a stranger at the carefree vision of children playing nearby, or simply admiring someone's being, by connecting with others, we are also connecting with ourselves in a much more real sense. In acceptance, we can't help but find joy and peace.

On our journey to create *Be...a Woman*, Arline and I have met some incredible women. Some we encountered on a streetcar, others in a hospital waiting room. Some names came to us in the form of referrals from other women who heard what we were doing and said, "Oh you have to meet my friend." We realized that the admiration we have for one another is truly outstanding and that we must cultivate it. We are all sisters, mothers, and friends. We can all learn from each other. We love that we can be so strong and yet so vulnerable. We love that we can immediately open ourselves up to strangers and share life stories. We love that we feel emotionally free to cry when we are deeply touched by the lives of other women.

We have taken this experience with us, off these pages and into our lives. Our journey has just begun. We are full of curiosity and admiration as we observe women in everyday moments of life. The simple tasks we perform are muted in comparison to the joy that fills our souls as we engage in life, acknowledge our strengths, and commit to simply being ourselves...being transformed by the awareness of our own grace and allowing a new definition of beauty to evolve. Thank you for inspiring us!

...enjoy...

With love, Arline and Kim

With love and admiration,
we dedicate this book
to the memory of our mothers.

Arline and Kim

Glorious

Each new day

awakens in me the glory

of my true potential to face

the world with every ounce

of who I am.

Strong

Beneath the skin lies a soul

of great depth

that can only be seen as light,

that can only be felt as love,

that can only exist in me.

Reflective

The window of my soul reflects the sun,
provides a shield from the pain,

washes clean with tears.
It is the internal divide

between what is seen on the outside,
and what exists on the inside.

Knowing

Look into my eyes

and imagine what I have seen.

Gaze upon my smile

and hear the words that I have cried.

It is the wealth of knowing ourselves

through our experiences

that casts a magic spell on us.

Life teaches us what we know

in a language we all understand.

Generous

With my heart and with my hands,

I bind the fabric of our lives to create

warmth and comfort,

with threads of love not gold.

When I have tenderly touched

each woven inch,

I pass it on as a gift shared

between two, forever.

Loving

With every sense my body awakens,

I breathe him in,

I melt into his warm embrace.

I am fully present, yet caught up in the

intoxication of my dreamy, surreal emotions.

I love him, and I am loved by him,

and so love grows.

Hips

Encased by the rounded beauty of her hips, held up by the strength of her shape,
she is as unique as a handcrafted sculpture…never forcing life but allowing it to mold her.

At times, she sits in quiet contemplation,
of the moment after, sometimes in anticipation of the moment that lay ahead,
most often though she is entranced by the sweet simplicity of the moment she is in.
Her gentle curves and soft skin flex to comply with the demands of the hour,
smooth and relaxed at rest, firm and controlled with movement,
delicately padded as she prepares to deliver all the newness of life.

At times, she moves…her hips become the perfect resting place
from which little eyes get a first view of the world as they dance to the beat of her rhythm.
Swaying side to side, she walks with the cadence of a woman eager
to explore the realm of the unknown.
She is guided by the internal torch of life and by her own natural curiosity.

Through days and weeks and years, she gains experience and her life takes on new shape.
Poised in the million moments that comprise her day,
she sits again as she sifts through the weight of emotions and feelings
that she and those around her express endlessly.
Ever sculpting herself anew, she is changed by life and life by her…she breathes it in,
molded ever so slightly to a new form. Always evolving, always beautiful,
the figure of a woman is something to behold.

Patient

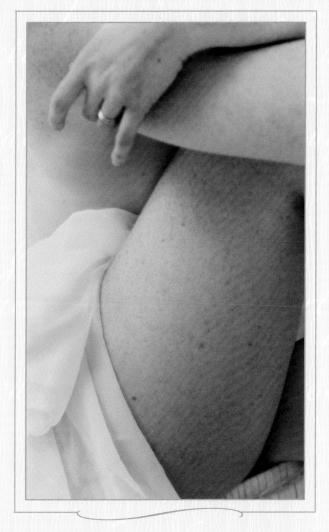

In reflection...I see my life unfold.
In peace...I hear my thoughts quiet themselves.
In stillness...I feel my heart pulse.
With patience, I become one with me, with the world.
There are no boundaries to contain my brilliant flight.

Mother

With every new challenge,

there are great victories

that come in tender whispers,

but none compare to

the birth of a mother.

Trusting

Listen…the music

echoes through me.

The brilliant beat of the rhythm

casts a shadow on my memories.

Though darkness surrounds me,

I reach for your hand,

I gain my balance,

your voice encircles me.

I am dancing through space.

In trust, I am reborn.

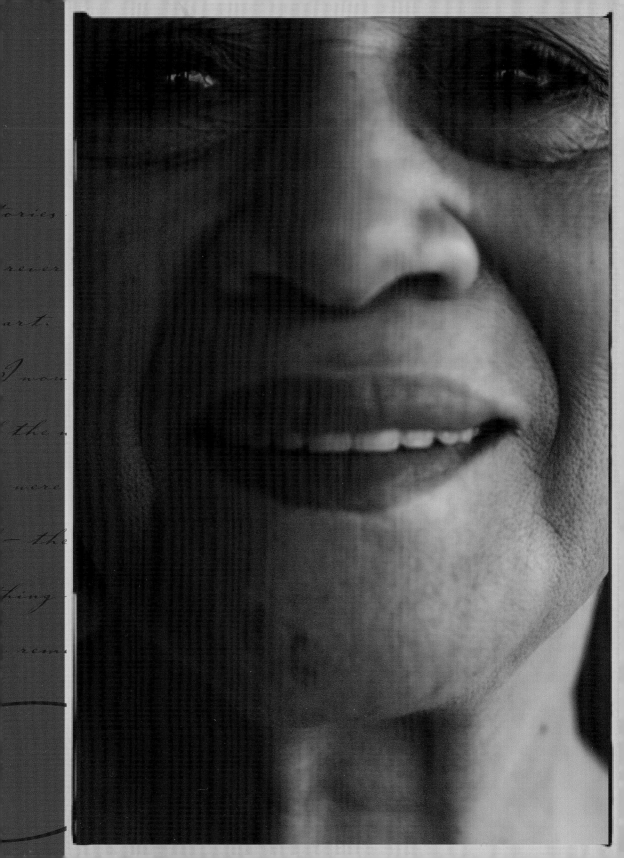

Radiant

Stripped of inhibition,

cocooned in the radiance of life,

warmed by the breeze of possibility that gently

brushes my skin,

I find peace within and hold it close.

INDIVID

Individual

I promise to be true to myself,

to turn away from judgment and cast aside fears.

I promise to find strength from within,

to surrender to happiness and admire individuality.

I promise to love who I am,

to accept myself and others for who they are.

Whether I am a daughter, a friend, a sister,

or a lover, I promise to always be me.

Forgiving

Neither perfection

nor imperfection

alone bring me joy;

it is acceptance of both

that make me whole.

Free of judgment,

I forgive.

In forgiveness,

I find grace.

Feet

If I were to add up all the steps she has taken to reach

where she stands today, I would get the chance to observe

the shape of her life in the footprints she has embossed on the world.

In the tender tiny toes that first taught her the power of movement,

I would see her sense of discovery at the side of every flower garden,

pebble, and pond. In the zigzagged imprint of her worn-out sneakers,

I would see the speed with which she tested her independence

from home to friends and back again.

In the elegant shape of her leather heels, I would see the confidence

with which she embarked on her career from office to promotions

and hard-earned raises.

In the warm glow of her naked feet, I would see her exploring passion

woven amidst her lover's embrace, from bed to beach to each tasty kiss.

In the gentle comfort of her swaying socked feet, I would see the love

she derives from experiencing the dance of life with a carefree child.

In the silent stillness of her rain-drenched boots, I would see the heartache

and compassion she shares standing next to a friend.

If I were to add up all the steps she has taken to

reach where she stands today, I would realize

she's not that different from me.

Resilient

Though I may stumble and fall,
I will always walk again, in a new direction,
with a new attitude, with a new resilience.

Observant

As I observe the world

around me through the lens

of an open soul,

the world unveils

its beauty in

luminous magnificence.

Courageous

A line is drawn between the shadows of darkness

and light, between what we know and what we fear.

Sometimes that line is blurred...it is in those times

that our inner resources guide us to safety.

Life acknowledges courage to be its strongest ally.

Nurturing

My hands are small,

but they can cradle life,

they can nurture dreams,

they can wipe away fears,

their strength is incomparable.

Earthy

Rooted in the warmth of the land

I reach toward the sky,

the sun, the moon.

I drift with the wind

and grow with the rain.

The heart of the Earth

beats within.

Capable

With my feet upon the ground…I tread.

With my hands to touch and hold…I feel.

Life has taken me to many places,

marked by the distance traveled,

measured both in miles and emotions.

In stillness…I catch my breath.

How capable I have been.

Peaceful

Days sometimes seem full of opposites.

Things that make sense collide with those

that confuse the logic of the mind.

Amidst the noise...

I listen for the hushed whisper of peace;

it fills me, surrounds me,

and brings me back to life.

Hands

The sound of her voice and the smell of her clothes have faded from my memory, but the touch of her hands – I remember those vividly. She had small, short fingers with a slight curve going up each. The skin on top was rough, the palms smooth as silk. She would gently caress my face to comfort, to praise, to admire what she had created.

Her expression took the place of words, it said, "You are wonderful. You are safe. You are loved." That simple, silent act instilled confidence, approval, and contentment in the soul of a young girl.

Did she ever understand the significance of her touch, I wonder?

Girls grow to be mothers. The lessons we learn are passed on to our children like heirlooms. I feel a familiar tingle inside, and a smile melts into my face as I run my hands over the soft, full skin of my little girl's rosy cheeks.

Creative

From the creation of ten perfect toes to the first fearless steps they take...

I am grateful for my hand in life's magnificent evolution.

Inspirational

There is something about the way her soul sings

that vibrates out to those around her.

With a simple look,

a gentle touch, a sweet smile,

a sense of spirit from deep within,

she inspires those around her to shine,

to live, to love, to be their best.

Fragile

I have seen more than I can understand.

I have cried more than my share of tears.

I have questioned more than I needed to ask.

I have struggled with more than simple fears.

I was just a girl, fragile and alone,

who has become a woman and is feeling

more at home, with me.

Sister

My eyes may be blue where yours are brown.

My hair may be straight where yours curls wildly.

My skin may be dotted with enough freckles

to rival a starry sky,

where yours is an even shade of milky tea.

To be sisters, we need not share

any special features,

we need only share a laugh, a tear, a hug…

a friendship that lasts forever.

...a friendship that lasts forever.

Yourself

We are leading ladies of our life's story.

Our wardrobe is only one element

of the fabric of our lives.

We direct ourselves

to perform with full emotion

and awareness in every moment.

And like any great story,

the legend that is "You"

emerges from the subtext.

Exuberant

The source of energy that pulses through my

veins has led me to a place of deep gratitude

and exuberance for life…

not because I bypassed the heartaches and tragedies

of youth but because I lived them. And so…

with spirit, heart, and a wicked sense of humor,

I can laugh in the face of adversity, knowing

I can summon the power from "with-in,"

so I will never be left "with-out."

Powerful

Miracles appear in the form of tiny angels

who allow us to experience our own power,

to reveal our own weakness,

to swell with unparalleled emotion

so that we may better know our true selves.

...a that we may better know

...ur true selves.

Back

Behind me lay a magnificent collection of moments,

choices made, new paths taken and left behind,

people I have come to know and some I have long forgotten.

Amidst the treasure chest of jewels, I find one constant

that has carried me through it all, one thing that holds me up,

even when it feels as if the very center of my being has been deflated.

There is one thing that summons strength – when I feel none…

that delivers courage – when I am frightened.

Often in the shadows, never knowing where I am headed until I have arrived…

it is the framework in which the story of my life records its history.

It gently hugs my heart, my breath, my soul,

protecting me from life's turbulence. Forever setting me straight.

It bears the burdens of weight and restlessness,

it forces me to stand for what I believe in,

to extend above to the sky and below to the earth.

Always supportive of every path I take and all the difference I make…

I am backed by its formidable grace and unshakable resolve.

Sensual

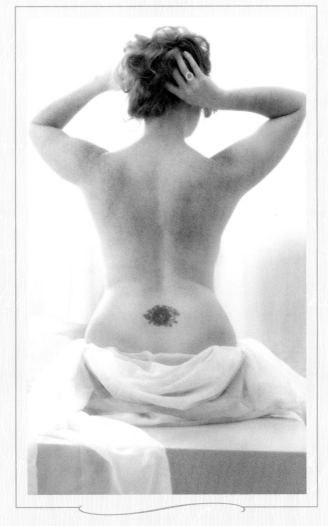

Cool air glides across each rounded edge of skin…caressing it…kissing it.
Warmed by the tender touch of fabric against my curves and the rising flame
ignited within…my senses awaken. I am beautiful. I am sensual.
I am ready to taste passion's sweet embrace.

Vibrant

Looking out at the world for decades,

I have seen so much, traveled so much,

loved and lost so much,

but I have never relinquished my sense

of childlike curiosity in life.

Ever vibrant, ever engaged,

life never fails to excite me.

Devoted

A union of hearts plants the seeds for growth

of minds and souls.

Cultivated for a lifetime, eyes speak without words

through experiences that could not be predicted.

Devotion blossoms and ties lovers together for eternity.

Intriguing

Quiet curiosity, a captivating gaze,

a face that transcends time and space.

I wonder if perhaps she was left behind,

a remnant of a distant world.

What stories would she dare to tell?

What secrets might she reveal?

Gentle

Tell me all your fears,

and I will dissolve them all with love.

Whisper to me your feelings,

and I will embrace them with respect.

Share with me your dreams,

and I will shower them with belief.

With a gentle smile, a hug, a word,

I will honor who you

are as I do myself.

Mysterious

Perfection is not nearly

as intriguing

as the mystery beneath

the veil of reality.

Wise

We are all travelers in life

composed of postcards

from different destinations.

Our faces reveal a snapshot

from every stop we've made

along our journey,

our message only

readable between the lines.

Mouth

She smiles...but with more than the curve of her

mouth. Her eyes narrow as if trying to capture inside

the feeling of joy that dances across her face.

It is like trying to shove a fluffed-up, worn sweater back

into its original package, it oozes out the sides.

Having stretched and experienced freedom, it now

refuses to conform to its previous state. Her smile

continually stretches beyond – up and around her face.

Soon her eyes twinkle like a thousand stars in the

nighttime sky. Her head arches back in the most

beautiful position, open, up. The chorus now joins in,

her ears sit a quarter of an inch back, her forehead reaches high.

Then the most wonderful sound...the breath.

She gathers more air into her lungs, the feeling

cascading down her shoulders, into her chest and arms.

Her entire body is involved now, the

crescendo of the piece reaches a laugh.

So unique, so distinct. Her laughter fills my soul.

Her smile warms my heart.

Joyful

Wrapped up in the unquantifiable beauty of the moment,
I embrace freedom, gratitude, and the goodness of life.
Guided neither by words nor actions but by unshakable resolve,
I am lifted above happiness to pure joy. In perfect harmony, I am aglow.
This is what it means to feel alive.

Journal Entry of Erika from Photo Shoot for "Courageous" and "Inspirational"

Once you meet Erika, you never forget her. A bubbling brew of life and enthusiasm combined with a speckled face of brilliant freckles gives the impression that she is much younger than twenty-nine. At ease in front of the camera, Erika settles into the studio with her usual air of confidence. In the past five years I have known her, she has become a huge part of my life and the lives of my three children. At her request, my girls are here to be part of her picture. They run to greet her as they all collide in a pool of giggles, hugs, and kisses. There is mutual love and friendship between them...kindred spirits all brought to life in each other's presence. The atmosphere in the studio is magical...the sun is beaming through the window, casting a prism of rainbow colors on the wall as it shoots through a crystal vase. Feeling the beauty of the moment, Arline begins to snap pictures. It is effortless and quick...the moment is captured faster than any other photo shoot. "I can see why you wanted the kids with you," Arline says. "You all look like a family." Erika smiles from inside the circle my little girls have formed around her. "I love kids!" she exclaims. "But I love these angels like my own. They give me hope and that extra push when I feel I have nothing left to give. They are my therapy...I call it munchkin therapy." I have heard Erika say these words many times before, but the impact of her statement today as my little "munchkins" dance around her brings me to tears. Diagnosed with stage-four colon cancer in March 2005, Erika's lifetime dream of pregnancy and motherhood has been taken away.

Courageous *Inspirational*

Endless rounds of chemotherapy have left her body too scarred and fragile to consider conceiving a child. In spite of physical and emotional pain that pushes her to the limit, Erika remains playful and optimistic. She is a study in courage…not the kind the Lion requested from the Wizard of Oz…but the kind that appears to be summoned effortlessly when great effort is demanded. There are times in every woman's life when what she dreams about seems off course with what she hoped for. Amidst the inevitable feelings of frustration, fear, and disappointment, Erika dares to keep hoping for more and dreaming new dreams of a life rich with love, marriage, and children. She stands by the window for a few solo shots…the glowing face of possibility. It doesn't surprise me that she has recently fallen in love, unaffected by the polarities simultaneously operating in her life she chooses to connect – lives intertwining – opening eyes to so many emotions…gratitude…respect…appreciation for the moment…for the beauty of life itself. The simple things that could be taken for granted – a friend, a partner, a laugh, a baby's cry – are the things Erika treasures most. I watch her listening to my children as they all speak to her at the same time, her smile reaches to every corner of the room. There is a musical celebration in the sound of their conversation. As Erika's life takes a slight detour down the cobblestone road, she skips, locking elbows with friends, leading them on a journey through the wonderful world of awes.

Journal Entry of Rani from Photo Shoot for "Knowing"

I met Rani through her daughter and a chance meeting we had at The Hospital for Sick Children. When I mentioned the book I was working on, she proudly said, "You have to meet my mom." It has been almost six months and we now have the privilege of meeting "Mom." She enters the studio with a rainbow of colorful saris thrown around her arm. She looks to me like a mixture of compassion, intelligence, and emotion. Although we have just met, she shares with us a traumatic childhood memory from her homeland in Pakistan that has clearly left its mark for life. The elegant woman standing before us was once an innocent seven-year-old whose world was forever changed when she witnessed the massacre of several family members. As she speaks, tears gently stream down her cheeks and her voice trembles with all the emotion of that frightened little child. I have been touched by stories and movies of genocide, but hearing about it now, as we can almost feel her heart pounding in the hollows of her chest, lifts it off the pages and leaves it deeply embedded in my own heart. We are captured by her story, her emotion, and her efforts to help other women who are victims of violence. This woman, who came from a distant country with her husband and only a few hundred dollars cash, a new baby, and very little understanding of the language and vastly different culture – this woman knows something about survival, about pain, and about overcoming hardships. We travel to the beach for our shot. The wind plays with Rani's hair. Birds dance above her as she stands under a towering tree that possibly rivals her age and wisdom. As Arline reloads her camera, Rani looks up toward the sky…the flapping wings of freedom…the reaching arms of the noble old tree…new tears cascading down her cheek. Arline poises her camera to shoot, then pauses to comfort our new friend. We move toward her protectively to see if she's all right. "I just feel so special right now. You girls have made me feel so beautiful. Thank you for allowing me to share my life with you." This moment of gratitude is like the beauty of her teardrops. There is no beginning and no end…something created from emotion…cleansing as it touches…skin…hearts. I can't help but realize that knowing about someone else's journey in life enriches our own to no end and connects us for eternity. I am filled with deep admiration and respect for this woman, who says she still feels she has so much to do in the world to make a difference. Perhaps those differences are made in the sweet simplicity of shared moments.

09 • 23 • 2006

Knowing

Journal Entry of Paula from Photo Shoot for "Mother" and "Earthy"

As I watch my friend Paula play with baby Lola on the beach, I am caught up in the surrealism of the moment. A perfect little baby…a perfect mommy…a perfect moment in time. Paula, like any new mom, has had to adapt to a whole new life with this tiny creation now dominating her world. This stunning image hides the face of a woman struggling to make sense of her roles of wife and mother. With her baby, giggles and kisses have teetered endlessly beside groans and tears, and "unconditional love" has now been perfectly defined. With her husband, one-time lovers and best friends have somehow become fatigued, awkward strangers. The birth of this little baby and the magnitude of the demands of motherhood, though challenging, feel effortless alongside the simultaneous death of the love affair she treasured with her husband. Carefree, inseparable partners have become fragile drifters caught in the winds of change…headed in different directions…held together by the unique little person created from their pure love. The battle of mixed emotions runs high in the face of this incredible shift in life for Paula. One moment, she is filled with joy and elation experiencing life with Lola. The next moment, she is immersed in fear as the limits of her marriage are tested and the uncertainty about the future of her new "family" threaten with the consideration of single parenthood. Throughout the years, Paula and I have exchanged advice and wisdom in various areas of our lives, but I realize that no measure of words could ever truly prepare us for the role of mother and the inevitable shift in the role of wife. It must simply be experienced to be understood. The illusion of perfection is shattered and replaced by a deep respect for the unexpected challenges of reality. Then like an unspoken treasure we all own a fragment of, we look at each other differently, respect each other immensely, and defer to the life of the little people to help us expand and grow and become our very best. The struggle to find balance between husband and child starts to settle as we all grow together and find peace with the new dynamic of our families. Paula glances my way and smiles as Lola grows impatient and opts instead to test the grains of powder that tease her feet. Instinctively, I reach out and offer Paula relief. As we complete the hand-off, she says to Arline and me, "Being a part of this book is such a gift for Lola; I wish I could remember all of this with my mom. Only now do I fully understand how much she gave me and how much she gave up for me." The mystery of motherhood truly does reveal itself in the myriad of hushed kisses that linger in the recesses of the mind, kisses given to us by our mothers, our lovers, and those bestowed upon our babies.

08 - 06 - 2006

Earthy *Mother*

Journal Entry of Katrina from Photo Shoot for "Trusting"

Katrina, the graceful blonde regally looking toward
the camera, was a professional dancer in Australia.
Four years ago, at the age of forty, she lost complete vision,
bringing an abrupt end to a career she loved so much.
This photo shoot was the first time she had danced in
four years. Katrina's dance partner, Anoush,
graciously volunteered to guide Katrina through her
moves. None of us really knew what to expect, but we
all felt like we were part of something groundbreaking!
Though we weren't landing on the moon, that sunny
afternoon it felt like "one small step for man…one giant
leap for mankind." It was also a bonding of two women
who had never met before but who shared a common love
of dance. In this intimate encounter, it was as if they had
been best friends, as if they were comrades – two graceful
birds connecting through touch, voice, and heart. I couldn't
help but look around and acknowledge the beauty of this
moment. Katrina's two sidekicks watched on: her loving
husband sat back, quietly enjoying watching the freedom of
his wife perform, while her yellow lab guide dog cried and
jumped anxiously trying to protect his partner from movements
he seemed unfamiliar and concerned with. Arline and I
were moved to tears to witness the grace and elegance she
displayed and ultimately the trust in letting go of the darkness
and reaching for that faded memory of light. Her body quickly
regained its composure and no one would have known she couldn't
see a thing. A marvel to watch, the beauty of her spirit and
determination radiates in this image.

12 - 9 - 2006

Journal Entry of Hannah from Photo Shoot for "Fragile" and "Loving"

Hannah enters the studio with an aura of shyness and apprehension. The girlfriend of Michael, our videographer, she is symbolic of the younger category of "emerging woman." Her sparkling green eyes seem to radiate a mixture of naiveté and experience. Michael kisses her goodbye and heads out to finish his Christmas shopping. As Arline scans all the brilliant hues in Hannah's selection of clothes, it is her flawless, fresh skin that she is drawn to. Hannah, the picture of youth and beauty, was nervous to be so exposed. The sense of vulnerability and discomfort in our own skin is a feeling most women can all relate to at some time. Hannah sits with her bare back to the camera. "Isn't it wonderful to be so young?" Arline says. Hannah turns, looking over her shoulder and counters, "No, I am happy to be leaving my youth behind." It strikes me as ironic that the much sought-after look of youth and beauty that is sold to us through the media as the answer to all life's problems was the very thing this young woman was trying to escape. Hannah being the daughter of a single mother who was addicted to drugs, her story of a childhood of responsibility, confusion, and fear begins to unfold. A young girl at the mercy of her mother's irrational mind-altering states surely carried an enormous weight on her tiny shoulders. It is unfathomable to consider the fear Hannah dealt with daily as drug dealers and strange men came in and out of the house while her mother was in no condition to protect her. No wonder she wants to claim womanhood and say goodbye to childhood – it was a door she lingered at long before she should ever have known about its existence. At twenty years old, Hannah has already lived a lifetime few women twice her age could comprehend. Arline is clearly moved by Hannah's confession and captivated by her candor. "That experience has made me who I am." Hannah declares. "No it hasn't, it only tested you," Arline responds. "You have emerged pure…as you." In the moment, the exchange of words, emotions, vulnerabilities, and revelations strikes me as so real and raw… this is truth…this is life: a fine balance of running from what we are…while others struggle to run toward what it appears on the outside they want to be…the desire to leave behind what we have lost and to find what we have not yet become. The innocence of her face captures my imagination. The fragility of the human spirit lingers in Hannah's eyes, as I think it does in all women at different times in our lives. How interesting that the very experience of fragility creates its opposite: strength. The metamorphosis of womanhood is beautiful in all its stages. Michael returns. Hannah flies to him and lands in his arms: a sigh of relief…a perfect fit…a final gift…a snapshot of love.

Fragile

Loving

Journal Entry of Maria from Photo Shoot for "Mysterious"

This mysterious image is universal and timeless.

A young woman hops on the streetcar.

Arline wants to photograph her.

"Why me?"

"Because I find you so beautiful," Arline replies.

She allows Arline to see her beauty…

Arline allows her to feel beautiful.

In spite of the awkwardness of the situation –

a busy streetcar…a rainy day…people coming and going…

the young woman's shyness – they connect with few words.

She misses her stop for Arline to take her picture.

Arline touches her hair. "Please don't…my hair is dirty."

Arline reaches across and puts her hood on…smiling at her.

The young woman turns away towards the window…

the shutter is triggered. A Madonna is born.

A mother…unemployed…her name was Maria…

we will never know more. Laced with gold and tied with ribbons…

delivered in the final moments of a brief journey together…

stunning gifts like this one hide in faces around us everyday.

09-10-2004

Mysterious

Journal Entry of Kazuko from Photo Shoot for "Peaceful"

Taking part in the festivities of the Japanese New Year, Arline and I enjoy the unexpected beauty of women dressed in traditional kimonos. Navigating the center through brilliant colors, smells, and sounds, we are both drawn to a woman engaged in a conversation. Above her navy blue kimono, just below her black hair, floats a pale face painted only with the brush of a smile. She has an aura of light around her…the illusion of an angel. As we approach her, she greets us with her eyes and instantly we connect…there is softness in her expression…gentleness… and a sense of undeniable strength. Without hesitation, she agrees to have her picture taken. It is as if she was waiting for us. Arline guides her to a window… the brilliance of the day shines through, yet it is her light that beams brightest. "May I ask your name?" Arline inquires. "My name is Kazuko," she replies, a faint Japanese accent lingers behind her words. "In my country it means 'peace.' I was born just after the war in Hiroshima. My parents gave me my name because they wanted to bring peace back into the world." The mother of a boy with severe autism, Kazuko feels overwhelmed by the responsibility of caring for a child with special needs. She questioned the fairness of life as she battled an internal war she felt she could not win. Then, in an instant, everything changed when a friend of Kazuko's visited a spiritual healer and told her that Kazuko had breast cancer. After some skepticism and a visit to the doctor, the diagnosis was confirmed. The early discovery led to treatment and a complete recovery. Standing face to face with Kazuko, Arline's eyes fill with tears as she lowers her camera. Kazuko takes her hand and says, "How could she have known?" Her voice is still fresh with the lingering mystery of revelation. "Someone I had never met saw something so seemingly invisible. That experience opened my eyes, my heart, my soul to life. It made me understand that the only real connection is to the above." She looks deeply into Arline's eyes and repeats the lesson. "The only real connection is to the above…don't forget that. Everything else is an illusion. Now I enjoy every drip of love and I realize my son is a blessing. He is the light of my life. My illness was a blessing. I am changed," she says, tears dripping down her porcelain cheeks. Arline's beret is cocked to one side, her camera rests on her hip, her cheeks too glitter with tears. She is awaiting the results of a mammogram. Together they have created an unexpected magic that fills the air. Kazuko slips a beautiful pink crystal ring from her finger and places it on Arline's. Hands intertwine…hearts connect …tears flow. "Keep this as a reminder of the power of connection. Let it bring you peace. Remember what surrounds you is an illusion…what is within you is life." This image reflects the simple, ageless face of an angel who realized she was only a breath away from a state of peace…she has fulfilled her prophecy…she has brought peace into the world. She is a messenger.

1 - 28 - 2007

Peaceful

laughter

Joined in mutual reverence.

Bonded through shared experiences.

Enduring the heartaches and joys of a lifetime

through laughter and tears,

in only the ways that matter.

Allowing life to guide us,

allowing our hearts to greet you,

whoever you are,

you are a friend to us,

you are a sister,

we are one.

To continue your journey
please visit our website at
www.be-awoman.com to review:

• Additional information on our other products.

• Information about our seminars,
both personal and corporate.

• Special ordering information for multiple
gift purchases of the book.

Please share your thoughts with us.
We want to know how this book has affected you.
Go to our site at www.be-awoman.com
and join the conversation
on our message board.

Help us get the message out about the
true beauty of womanhood.
Please go to www.amazon.com
and write a review of this book.